Clara Lidström

and

Annakarin Nyberg

LET'S BAKE

A Step by Step Introduction

With illustrations by Katy Kimbell & Li Söderberg
Translated by Viktoria Lindbäck

Let's Bake: A Step by Step Introduction

by Clara Lidström and Annakarin Nyberg
Translation from Swedish by Viktoria Lindbäck
Illustrations by Katy Kimbell and Li Söderberg

Published by Little Gestalten, Berlin 2015
ISBN: 978-3-89955-751-0

Typefaces: Consolas by Lucas de Groot; Mirabelle by Jessica
McCarty; Core Circus by Hyun-Seung Lee, Dae-Hoon Hahm,
and Min-Joo Ham

Printed by Livonia Print, Riga. Made in Europe.

The Swedish original edition Baka was published by Rabén &
Sjögren, Sweden 2014. © Clara Lidström and Annakarin Nyberg
© for the English edition: Little Gestalten, an imprint of Die
Gestalten Verlag GmbH & Co. KG, Berlin 2015

All rights reserved. No part of this publication may be reproduced
or transmitted in any form or by any means, electronic or mecha-
nical, including photocopy or any storage and retrieval system,
without permission in writing from the publisher.

Respect copyrights, encourage creativity!

For more information, please visit little.gestalten.com.

Bibliographic information published by the Deutsche Nationalbibliothek. The Deutsche Nationalbibliothek lists this publication in
the Deutsche Nationalbibliografie; detailed bibliographic data are
available online at http://dnb.d-nb.de.

This book was printed on paper certified by the FSC®.

FSC
www.fsc.org

MIX
Paper from
responsible sources
FSC® C002795

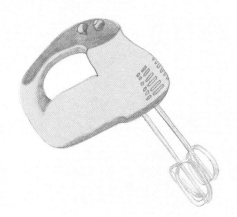

Table of Contents

Tips and a Few Other Things

This is a book for people who like to bake and do crafts in the kitchen. It's not a book for grown-ups. The point is actually that they should stay away as much as possible! Until you have to put a baking sheet in a hot oven, use the electric whisk, stove, or do anything else that might require their help!

Get started:

1) Choose a recipe.

2) Read through the recipe and take out all the ingredients you need.

3) Also take out the tools that you need: for example, bowls, spoons, measurements, tablespoons, and teaspoons.

4) Put on an apron and wash your hands.

Have the grown-ups left the kitchen yet? Good, let's go!

RASPBERRY FLUFF

We used raspberries for our fluff.
You can also use strawberries, blueberries,
or any other berries you like.

TAKE OUT:

berries

lime

1 lime

60 grams berries
(fresh or frozen)

90 grams plain
cream cheese

1 egg (just the white)

3 tablespoons sugar

60 grams berries
for decoration
(fresh or frozen)

berries for
decoration

SUGAR

sugar

egg

CREAM CHEESE

cream cheese

Limes are not just delicious—they also help against the itchy feeling of a mosquito bite. Just spread some lime juice on it!

Yum

HERE'S HOW YOU DO IT:

1 Wash the lime and dry it with tissues or a kitchen towel.

2 Grate ¼ of the green peel (use the side with the smallest holes). It may not seem like enough but it provides a lot of flavor. Don't use too much!

90 grams

3 Mix the lime peel, berries, and cream cheese in a bowl.

1 piece

4 Ask a grown-up to help you crack the egg and separate the yolk from the white.

5 Also ask them to help with the electric whisk. Beat the egg white in a bowl for about 3 minutes at a high speed. The egg white should become white and foamy.

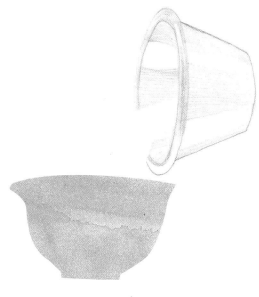

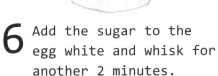

6 Add the sugar to the egg white and whisk for another 2 minutes.

7 While stirring, add the sugar and egg white mixture to the bowl with the berries and cream cheese. Mix it thoroughly.

8 Pour the fluff into four glasses and add some berries on top. Let the raspberry fluff cool off for an hour before you taste it!

If you place the glasses in the freezer, the fluff will turn into ice cream! But keep in mind that you should choose glasses that can handle the cold. The best glasses should never sit in the freezer.

CHEESECAKE IN A GLASS

You can eat this dessert right away.
You can also let it sit in the refrigerator for
a couple of hours before eating it–that's how
we like to eat it!

TAKE OUT:

200 milliliters
heavy cream

60 grams sugar

120 grams frozen
or fresh berries
like strawberries,
raspberries, or
blackberries

5-6 digestive crackers

optional: berries
for decoration
(fresh or frozen)

heavy cream

cream cheese

berries for decoration

strawberries

sugar

digestive crackers

Did you know that it
is more difficult to taste flavors
without the ability to smell?
Ask a friend to close their eyes
and hold their nose while you
feed him or her apples and
raw potatoes. They will
probably have a hard time
telling the difference!

HERE'S HOW YOU DO IT:

200 milliliters

200 grams

60 grams

1 Ask a grown-up to help you with the electric whisk. Beat the heavy cream in a bowl until it thickens.

2 Mix the cream cheese and sugar in a different bowl.

3 Add the cream to the cream cheese and sugar mix while stirring. Mix thoroughly so the batter becomes smooth.

120 grams

4 Let the frozen berries defrost until they become soft. Mash the berries with a fork in a bowl and add the berry mash to the batter. Taste some of the batter with a spoon— isn't it delicious?

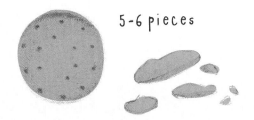

5-6 pieces

5 Crumble the digestive crackers with your hands

6 Take out four glasses. Add some crumbles at the bottom and add the batter on top. At last you add another layer of crumbles and then top off the glass with batter. If you want, you can add a couple of berries on top of each glass.

CHOCOLATE BALLS

The butter should be soft when you make these balls, so start by taking that out immediately. That will make it easy to work with. The coffee is not necessary but we think it's delicious! Ask a grown-up for some cold coffee.

about 30 balls

TAKE OUT:

cocoa

vanilla sugar

100 grams butter (soft)

100 grams sugar

130 grams oatmeal

1 teaspoon vanilla sugar

3 tablespoons cocoa

2 tablespoons cold coffee

coconut flakes, pearl sugar, or sprinkles

oatmeal

coffee

sugar

sprinkles

butter

Do you want to make your own sprinkles? Simply mix granulated sugar and food coloring in a bowl.

HERE'S HOW YOU DO IT:

100 grams

100 grams

130 grams

SUGAR

Oatmeal
HAVRE
GRYN

1 Cut the butter into pieces and add to a bowl. Add the sugar and oatmeal.

1 teaspoon

COCOA

3 tablespoons

2 tablespoons

2 Add the vanilla sugar and cocoa.

3 Add the coffee.

4 Knead everything together into a batter.

5 Form tiny balls from the batter.

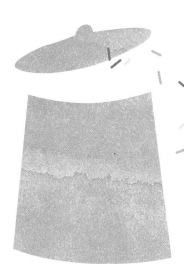

6 Add the coconut flakes, pearl sugar, or sprinkles to a plate and roll the balls in it.

Did you know that cocoa trees can grow 10 meters tall and that their fruits are filled with beans that you use to make chocolate?

QUICK CRISP COOKIES

When you make these yummy cookies, you need
to use the stove. Remember to always ask
a grown-up for help when it is time to use it!

15 cookies

TAKE OUT:

cornflakes

100 gram butter

80 grams sugar

4 tablespoons
light syrup

2 tablespoons cocoa

150 - 200 grams
cornflakes

syrup

muffin molds

butter

SUGAR

sugar

cocoa

HERE'S HOW YOU DO IT:

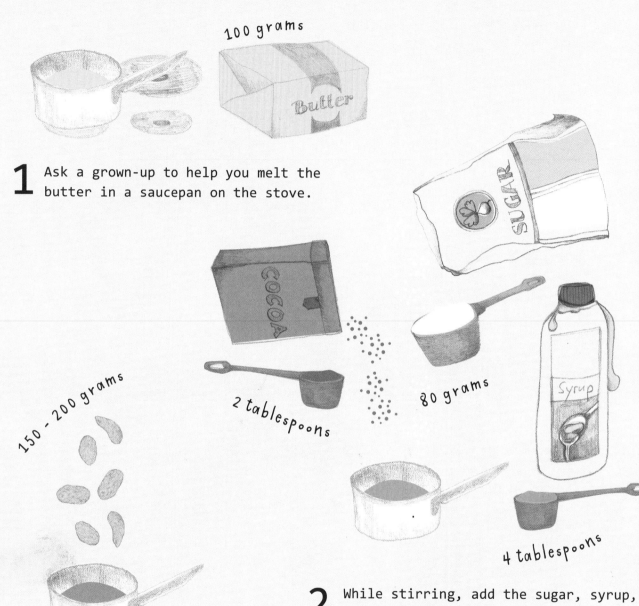

100 grams

Butter

SUGAR

COCOA

2 tablespoons

80 grams

Syrup

150 - 200 grams

4 tablespoons

1 Ask a grown-up to help you melt the butter in a saucepan on the stove.

2 While stirring, add the sugar, syrup, and cocoa to the saucepan along with t melted butter and let the mix carefull simmer for a couple of minutes.

3 Remove the saucepan from the plate and add the cornflakes while stirring.

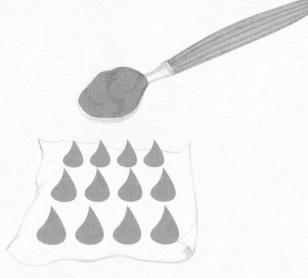

4 Take out a baking sheet and place little muffin molds on it. Carefully add the batter to the molds. If you don't have any muffin molds you can take greaseproof baking paper and make tiny blobs of batter.

Are the molds tipping over when you add the batter? Grease the bottom of the baking sheet with oil to make them stick.

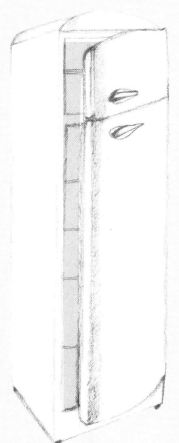

5 Refrigerate the baking sheet or put them in the freezer and let them sit for 30 minutes.

FUDGE COOKIES

Fudge cookies are delicious to eat on their own and they are also great to serve with ice cream like we did in the picture. Yummy!

baking powder

TAKE OUT:

about 30 cookies

100 grams butter

80 grams sugar

160 grams flour

1 tablespoon vanilla sugar

1 teaspoon baking powder

1 tablespoon light syrup

flour

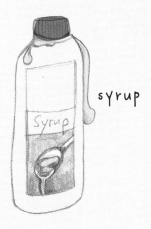

syrup

butter

sugar

vanilla sugar

26

Did you know that a human eats about 70 tons worth of food during his or her lifetime-equal to the weight of 14 elephants!

100 grams

80 grams

1 Take out the butter so that it has time to become soft. Ask a grown-up to help you set the oven to 175°C.

160 grams

1 tea spoon

1 tablespoon

Vanilla sugar

2 Place the butter in a bowl and add the sugar. Stir with a spoon so that it becomes a batter.

3 Mix the flower, vanilla sugar, and baking powder in a separate bowl.

4 Add the mixture to the butter and sugar batter.

5 Add the syrup.

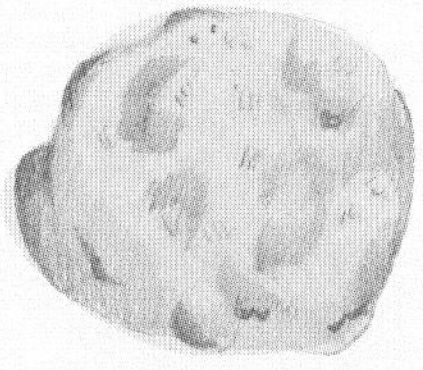

6 Knead everything together into a dough.

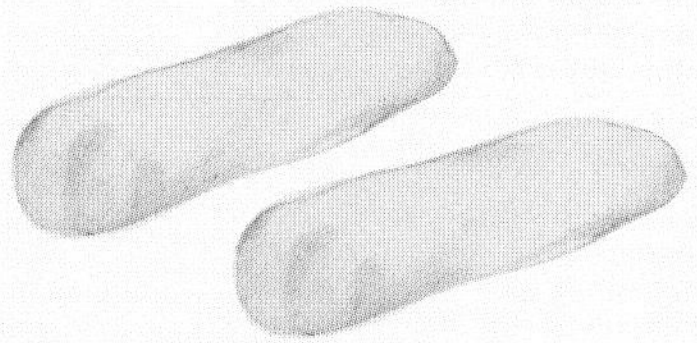

7 Split the dough into two pieces and shape them into rolls. They should be about two centimeters thick.

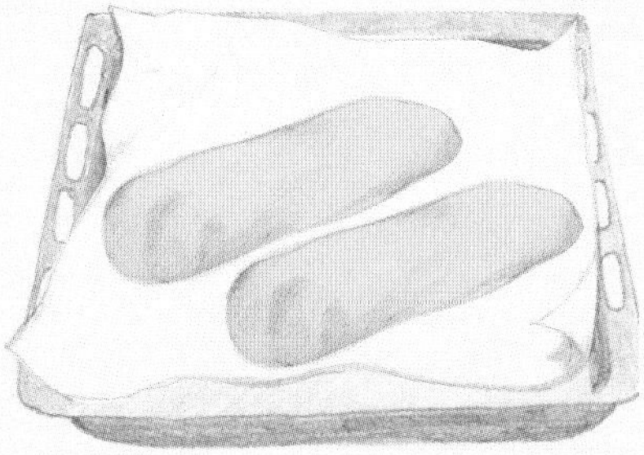

8 Place the rolls on a baking sheet with a greaseproof paper. Ask a grown-up for help with putting the baking sheet in the middle of the oven. Bake for 10-12 minutes.

9 Ask a grown-up to remove the baking sheet from the oven. Cut the rolls into cookies while they are still hot. Let the cookies cool on the baking sheet.

SHORTCRUST COOKIES

The image shows three different cookies. Although they look different from each other, they are made from the same dough called shortcrust pastry. Which kind do you want to make? Perhaps you can even make up your own kind?

TAKE OUT:

about 30 cookies

300 grams flour

80 grams sugar

200 grams butter (soft)

jam, like strawberry or raspberry

chopped sweet almonds

sugar

raspberry jam

sweet almonds

flour

butter

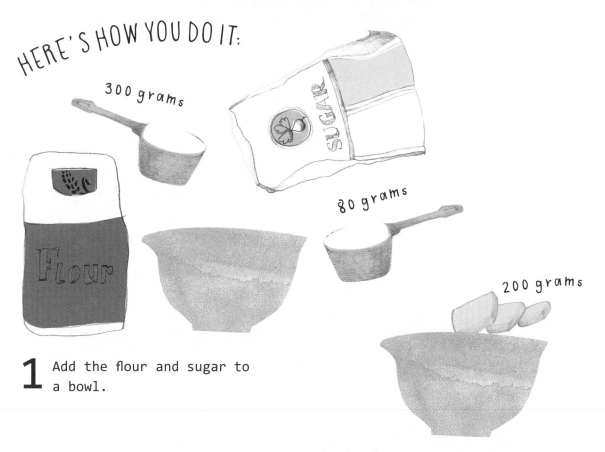

300 grams

SUGAR

Flour

80 grams

200 grams

1 Add the flour and sugar to a bowl.

2 Cut the butter into little pieces, add them to the bowl, and knead it together to form a dough.

3 Make two rolls. They should be three centimeters thick.

4 Put the rolls in a plastic bag and let them rest in the refrigerator for 30 minutes.

5 Ask a grown-up for help to set the oven to 175°C.

6 Take out the rolls from the refrigerator and cut into pieces. Choose what kind of cookies you want to make.

With jam: Make indentations in the cookie using your thumb and add jam.

With sweet almonds: Ask a grown-up for help with chopping the almonds. Dip the cookies in the chopped almonds so that the almond pieces stick to them.

Striped: Press a fork on top of the cookies.

7 Take out a baking sheet and place a greaseproof paper on top.

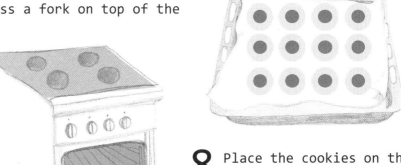

8 Place the cookies on the baking sheet and bake them in the middle of the oven for 10 minutes. Ask a grown-up for help!

BLUEBERRY MUFFINS

Feel free to try baking with different kinds of berries!
Just remember that big berries like strawberries must be
cut into smaller pieces.

blueberries

about
8-10 muffins

TAKE OUT:

eggs

2 eggs

120 grams sugar

1 teaspoon vanilla sugar

100 grams butter

200 milliliters milk

250 grams flour

2 teaspoons baking powder

½ pinch salt

120 grams blueberries
(fresh or frozen)

salt

vanilla sugar

SUGAR

sugar

milk

flour

butter

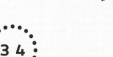

baking powder

34

Get eagle eyes
with blueberries!
They are said
to enhance
your sight.

HERE'S HOW YOU DO IT:

2 pieces

1 teaspoon

SUGAR

120 grams

1 Ask a grown-up for help with setting the oven to 175°C.

2 Crack the eggs in a bowl. Add the sugar and vanilla sugar.

100 grams

3 Ask for help with setting up the electric whisk. Whisk the eggs and sugar at a high speed for 2 minutes.

4 Melt the butter in a saucepan on the stove. Ask a grown-up for help.

200 milliliters

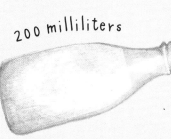

5 Add the milk and melted butter to the batter while stirring.

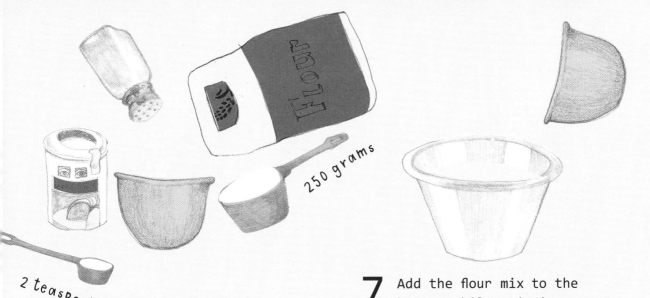

2 teaspoons

250 grams

6 Mix the flour, baking powder, and salt in a small bowl.

7 Add the flour mix to the batter while stirring.

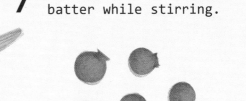

9 Push a teaspoon of blueberries into each muffin.

8 Place muffin molds on a baking sheet. You can also use a muffin specific baking sheet which makes the molds steadier. Fill the molds halfway up with batter.

11 Ask for help with removing the baking sheet from the oven. Let your muffins cool down before tasting them!

10 Ask a grown-up for help with placing the baking sheet in the middle of the oven. Bake for 12-15 minutes.

MUG CAKE

This is a really simple recipe! Just make sure that you have a microwave that you can use. If you want to decorate with berries, why not replace the milk chocolate with flavored chocolate?

milk

TAKE OUT:

1 serving

25 grams butter

4 tablespoons flour

1 pinch baking powder

2 tablespoons cocoa

1 egg

3 tablespoons milk

2 slices of a kind of chocolate that you like

flour

sugar

cocoa

baking powder

chocolate

egg

butter

HERE'S HOW YOU DO IT:

25 grams

Want to make decorations out of chocolate? Melt some chocolate in a saucepan, spread it out in thin shapes on a baking sheet, and place in the refrigerator to solidify.

1 Take out a big mug. Add the butter to the mug and melt it in the microwave. Ask a grown-up for help.

4 tablespoons

2 tablespoons

4 tablespoons

2 Mix the flour, baking powder, sugar, and cocoa in the mug.

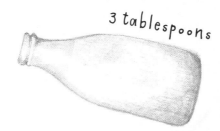

1 piece

3 tablespoons

3 Add the egg and milk. Mix carefully; it should become a smooth batter without lumps.

4 Add the pieces of chocolate and put the mug in the microwave.

Did you know that brown hens lay brown eggs and white hens lay white eggs? Ostriches also lay eggs. They are huge and weigh as much as two milk cartons!

5 Set the microwave to the highest temperature and bake for about 2½ minutes. Ask a grown-up for help!

HEDGEHOG CAKE

The Swedish started making this cake almost a hundred years ago and it is called radio cake there. At that time, the radio was a new invention and people thought it was a good idea to eat this cake while listening to the radio. Why? Well, because it doesn't make a crunching noise!

8-10 pieces

TAKE OUT:

250 grams coconut fat

7 tablespoons powdered sugar

2 eggs

3-4 tablespoons cacao

1 tablespoon vanilla sugar

1 packet crackers

eggs

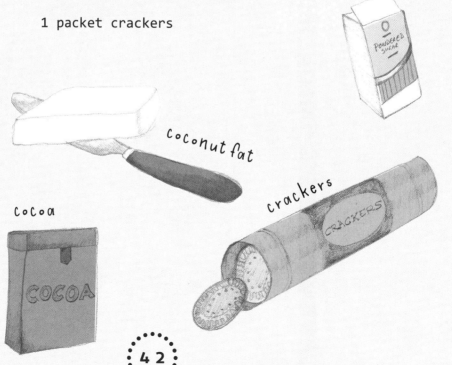

powdered sugar

coconut fat

crackers

vanilla sugar

cocoa

The cake in the photograph was made in a round mold. You can also use any other mold but it should have room for about 1½ liters.

HERE'S HOW YOU DO IT:

350 grams

7 tablespoons

1 Ask a grown-up for help with melting the coconut fat in a saucepan on the stove. Let the fat cool down.

2 Place a greaseproof baking paper on the kitchen table. Take out a dense strainer (ask a grown-up) and pour the powdered sugar through it so it falls on the paper.

2 pieces

3 Crack the eggs in a bowl and add the powdered sugar.

4 Ask a grown-up to help set up the electric whisk. Whisk the eggs and sugar at a high speed for 2-3 minutes. The batter is supposed to be fluffy.

1 tablespoon

3-4 tablespoons

COCOA

5 Add the cocoa and vanilla sugar and whisk it into a smooth batter.

6 When the coconut fat has cooled down, add it to the bowl and whisk until it becomes a smooth batter again.

7 Add a greaseproof baking paper to a mold and spread out a layer of the batter. Add a layer of crackers on top and keep going with a layer of each. Remember that the top layer should consist of batter.

8 Let the cake sit in the freezer for 2 hours so that it solidifies.

45

CURRANT PIE

This currant pie is also called crumble pie. It can be
filled with all sorts of delicious things like apples,
rhubarb, strawberries, or blueberries.
What would you like in your pie?

8-10
pieces

TAKE OUT:

baking powder

100 grams flour

120 grams oatmeal

80 grams sugar

1 teaspoon baking powder

100 grams butter

180 grams currants
(frozen or fresh)

currants

sugar

flour

Oatmeal

butter

HERE'S HOW YOU DO IT:

1 Ask a grown up for help with setting the oven to 200°C.

80 grams

120 grams

1 teaspoon

2 Mix the flour, oatmeal, sugar, and baking powder in a bowl.

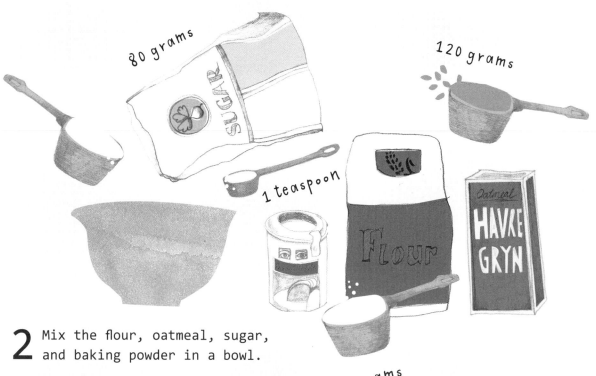

100 grams

100 grams

3 Cut the butter into little pieces and pinch it together with the flour mix until it becomes a crumbly dough.

300 milliliters

4 Put some butter on a greaseproof baking paper or butter a baking mold.

5 Place part of the dough in the pie mold. Sprinkle the berries on top and add the rest of the dough.

Have you ever considered that your tap water is the same water that the dinosaurs drank and the same water that the Vikings once sailed?

6 Ask a grown-up for help with placing the pie in the middle of the oven.

7 When 25 minutes have passed, it is time to take out the pie. Get help from a grown-up. Let the pie cool down for a while before you cut yourself a delicious piece. Ice cream, vanilla curd, or whipped cream is a great condiment.

Epilogue for Grown-ups

This is a book for children. A book that kids can use by themselves without too much involvement from us grown-ups. It is easy to end up hovering over your kids' shoulders and provide unwelcome comments and advice. Us adults are usually also too focused on the end result that we forget that the journey is the most important part.

With clear illustrations and easy recipes, we set out to create a baking book that, step by step, guides independent little bakers. Of course there are some elements that require help. That is inevitable when things need to be baked and whisked!

Our intention is for the recipes to act as suggestions: not the law. That leaves room for interpretation and hopefully the children can come up with their own takes on the recipes.

Your kitchen might become dirty from all the experimentation and you may have to try a piece of pie that is more salty than sweet. A lot of exciting things can happen when different ingredients are combined with independence and creativity. But we think that's the point—to try new flavors and learn new things!

Annakarin & Clara